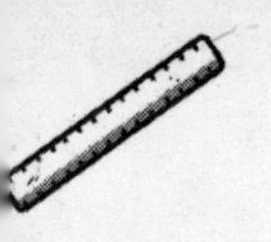

#ROF

Whatever the lesson, whate

we've got you covered with the silliest, funniest, craziest jokes in the world... ever! Your friends will be rolling around **LAUGHING** their heads off and the teacher won't be able to do anything about it, because they will be too!

And, if you share the jokes with your friends, and then they share them with their friends, and then they share them with their friends, pretty soon we will have created **PUNDEMONIUM**!

So, whether you prefer lols to laughs, or like your jokes as jks, then this is definitely the bk 4 u (and the book for you too)!

For Jonny Z. and Dave W.
- the funniest guys...

And thanks to everyone at
Award and James Cottell!

I.B.

To Mandy, thank you for what
you did for me all those years ago.
I am forever grateful.

To my friends and family, the Award
team and James for being awesome.

To R.E.M. for writing 'Everybody Hurts'.
I love that song.

S.V.

For every copy sold, Award Publications Limited
will make a £0.25 donation to Comic Relief,
which is the operating name of Charity Projects,
a registered charity in England and Wales
(326568) and Scotland (SC039730).

For more information, go to:
www.comicrelief.com

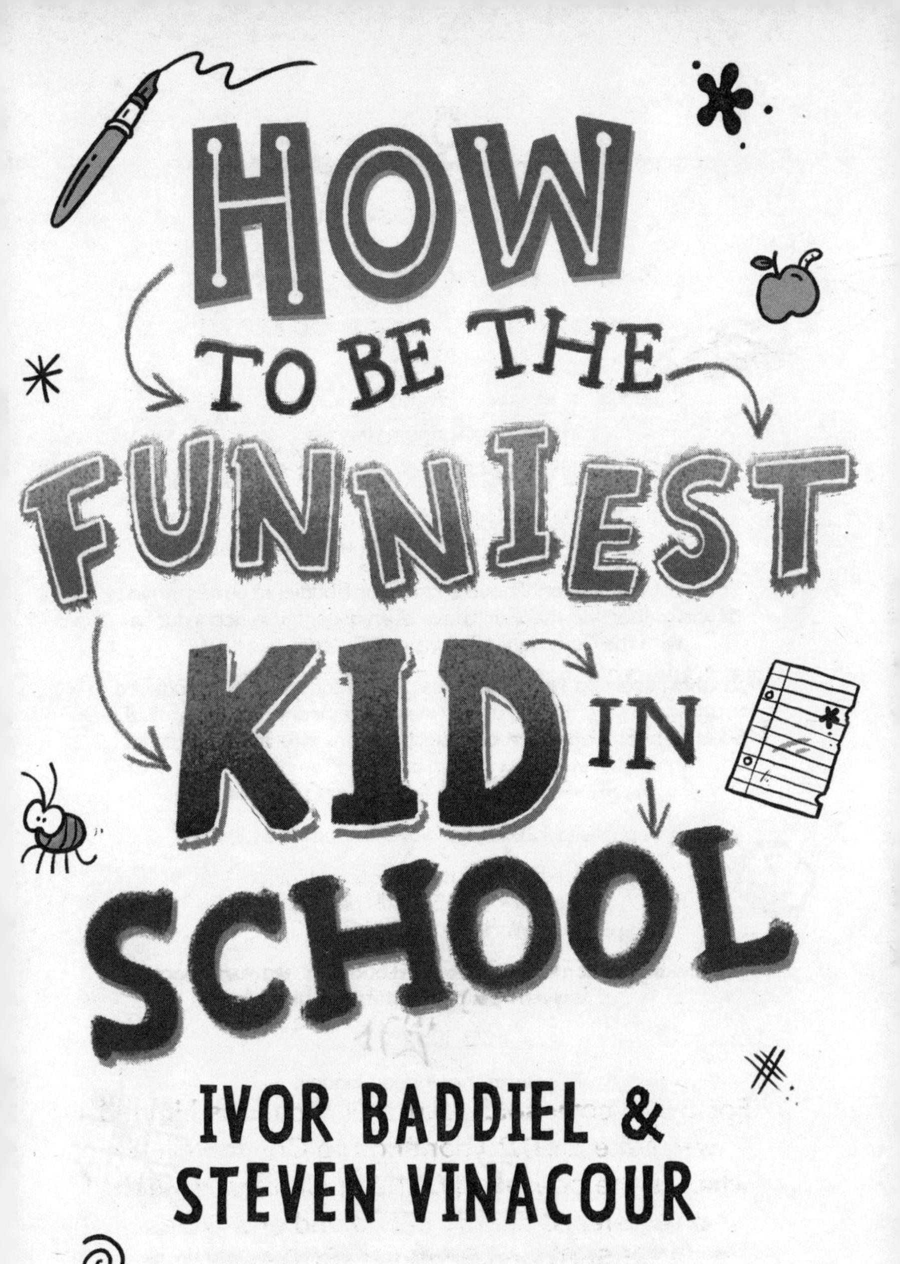

IVOR BADDIEL &
STEVEN VINACOUR

Illustrated by James Cottell

AWARD PUBLICATIONS LIMITED

ISBN 978-1-78270-533-8

Illustrations by James Cottell

First published 2023 by Award Publications Limited

Published by Award Publications Limited,
The Old Riding School, Welbeck,
Worksop, S80 3LR

/awardpublications @award.books @award_books
www.awardpublications.co.uk

23-1052 1

Printed in the United Kingdom

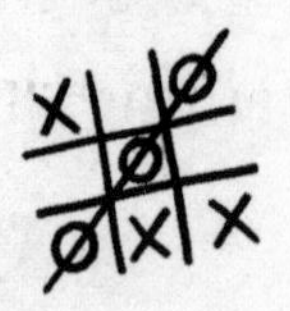

CONTENTS

INSTRUCTIONS

To be the funniest kid in school you will need:

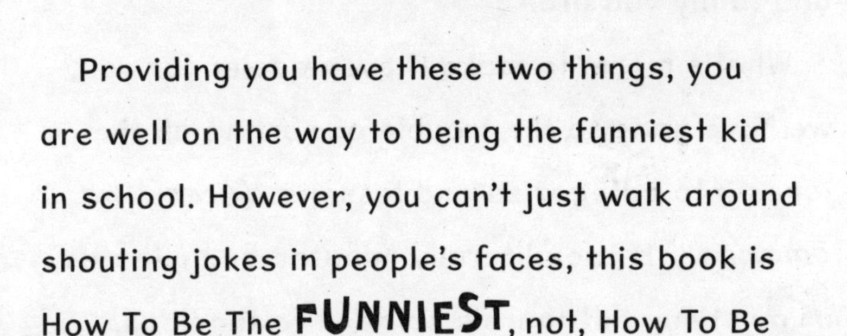

Providing you have these two things, you are well on the way to being the funniest kid in school. However, you can't just walk around shouting jokes in people's faces, this book is How To Be The **FUNNIEST**, not, How To Be The Most ***ANNOYING***.

So, there is a lot to consider:

The perfect joke needs perfect timing but, you also have to take other things into consideration like the mood of the pupils, the friendliness of your teacher, the time of day, what you had for lunch, the results from your

school sports team, the weather conditions and the position of the sun. Once you've studied all of these things then you'll know exactly the right moment to hit the class with your amazing joke, be crowned king or queen of comedy and be carried around the playground on a throne while your fellow pupils change the words of the school song to be about how amazingly great and funny you are.

What's more, to make it even easier for you, we have gone to the trouble of sorting all the jokes into categories and lessons. *(Aren't we amazing?)* It took literally minutes and minutes of our time, but there's no need to thank us. The only thanks we need is to hear the gales of **LAUGHTER** when you tell a belter in Biology or hit them with a humdinger at home time. (*And we will hear, we've got really, really good hearing*).

So study the jokes, pick your favourites and always be prepared *(like a Scout or Guide,*

only with fewer badges and more laughs) **(and no woggles, which is a very funny word but not a particularly funny thing).** Prepare yourself because your life is about to change.

Once, you were a reasonably funny kid who told the occasional joke, but now you are about to become...**(cue dramatic music)**

(No, more dramatic than that. Similar, but with more quiet bits and then loud drum bits!)

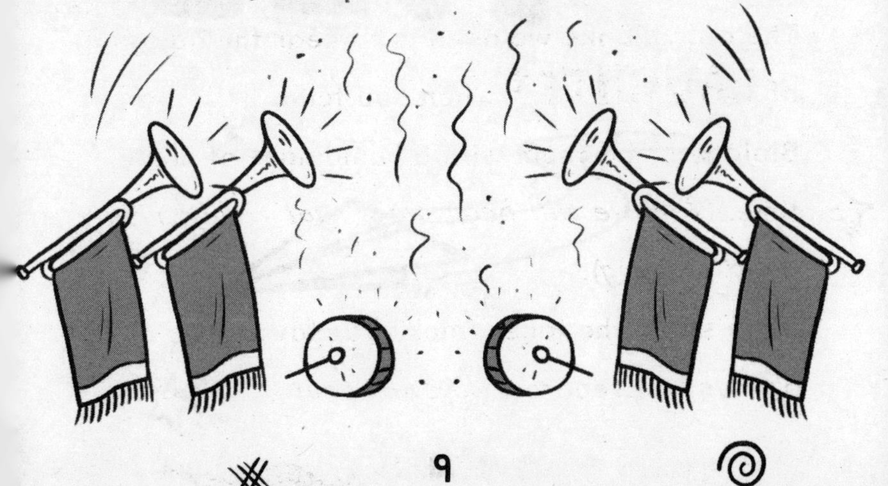

THE FUNNY KID

HA
HA
HA

*If more than one pupil in a school owns this book, then we aren't sure who becomes the funniest. To be honest, we haven't really thought this through properly.

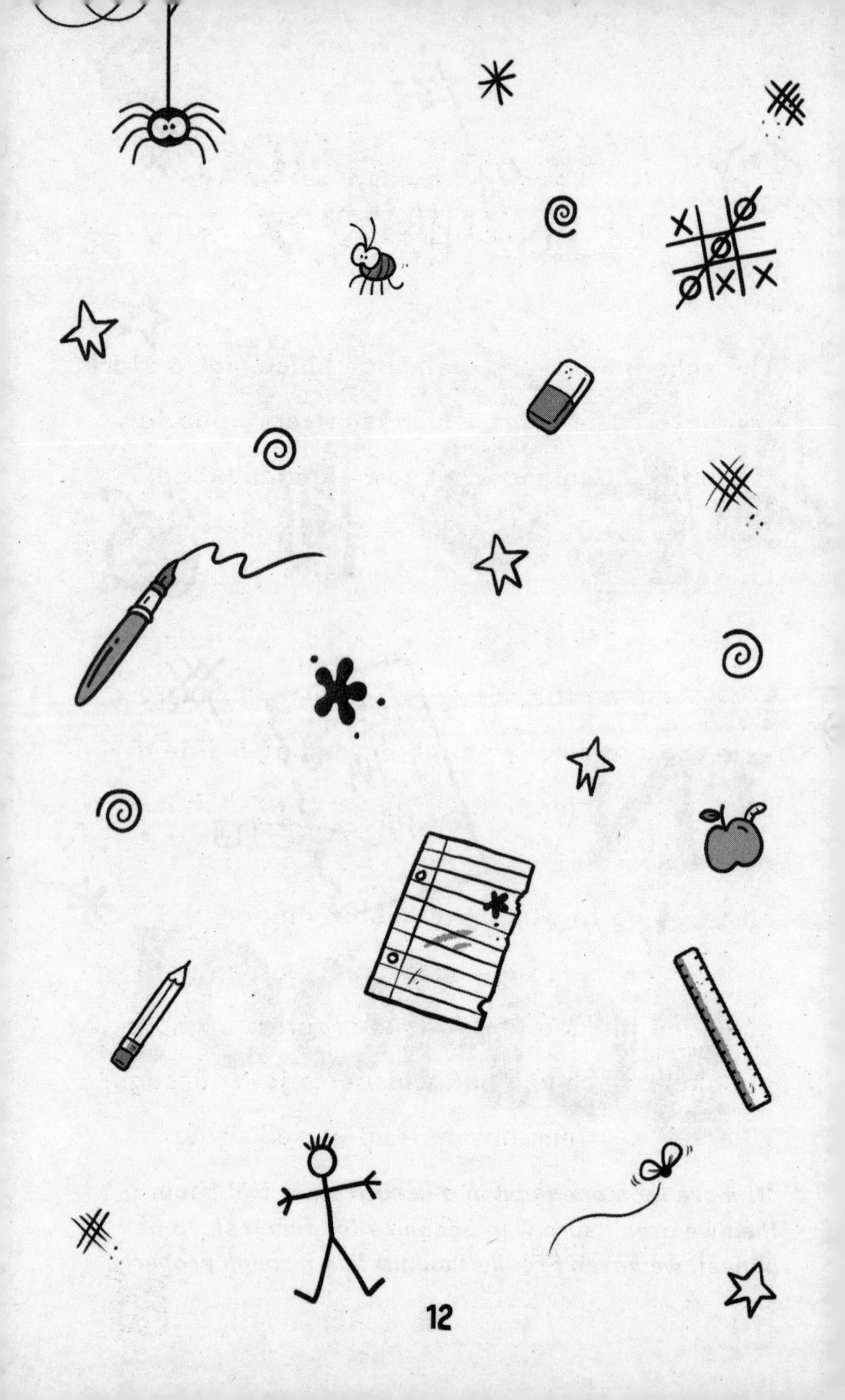

THE SCHOOL LIBRARY

The school library is a strange place. For a start you have to be quiet, which isn't very good for telling jokes unless you know sign language, or mime, or are telepathic – all of which you might be able to do, in which case, crack on and deliver the **FUNNIES**. If not, you are going to have to be a little sneaky about your delivery.

If you are small enough, try hiding inside a book and waiting until a reader gets to that page and then leaping out... hang on, that's never going to work. How about innocently browsing through the books and waiting until someone takes one out, thus creating a gap in the shelf which you can whisper a joke through? Like in a spy film, but instead of delivering the codes to a ***secret mission***, you tell them a knock knock joke.

Alternatively, you could try slipping this book into another much more educational book so that the teacher thinks you are very clever and says, ***'Well done, you must be incredibly smart reading that book. Have a house point,'*** when in fact you are reading this. Not that we are saying this book isn't clever. Some of the jokes are so clever we don't even understand them and we wrote them! But be warned, any noisy laughter that occurs in the library is guaranteed to get you a stern **'SHHHHH'** from the librarian.

By the way, we tried to plan a party in the school library but it was completely booked! No worries, instead we've taken out the best books for you to read.

HOW TO DRIVE A
POLICE CAR
BY
NINA NEENAR
COPING WITH DIARRHOEA
BY MARK D'PANTS
GARDENING TIPS
MO D'LAWN
PASTA RECIPES
BY PENNY ARABBIATA
BASIC FISHING TECHNIQUES
ANNETTE NEEDED
TRYING NOT TO GO TO THE TOILET DURING LESSONS
PHIL MAPANTS

FALLING OVER IN WINTER
TALKING IN CLASS
BECOMING AN INFLUENCER
A DAY OFF SCHOOL
Can't Hear the School Play
by Mike D. Actors
Silence in the Library

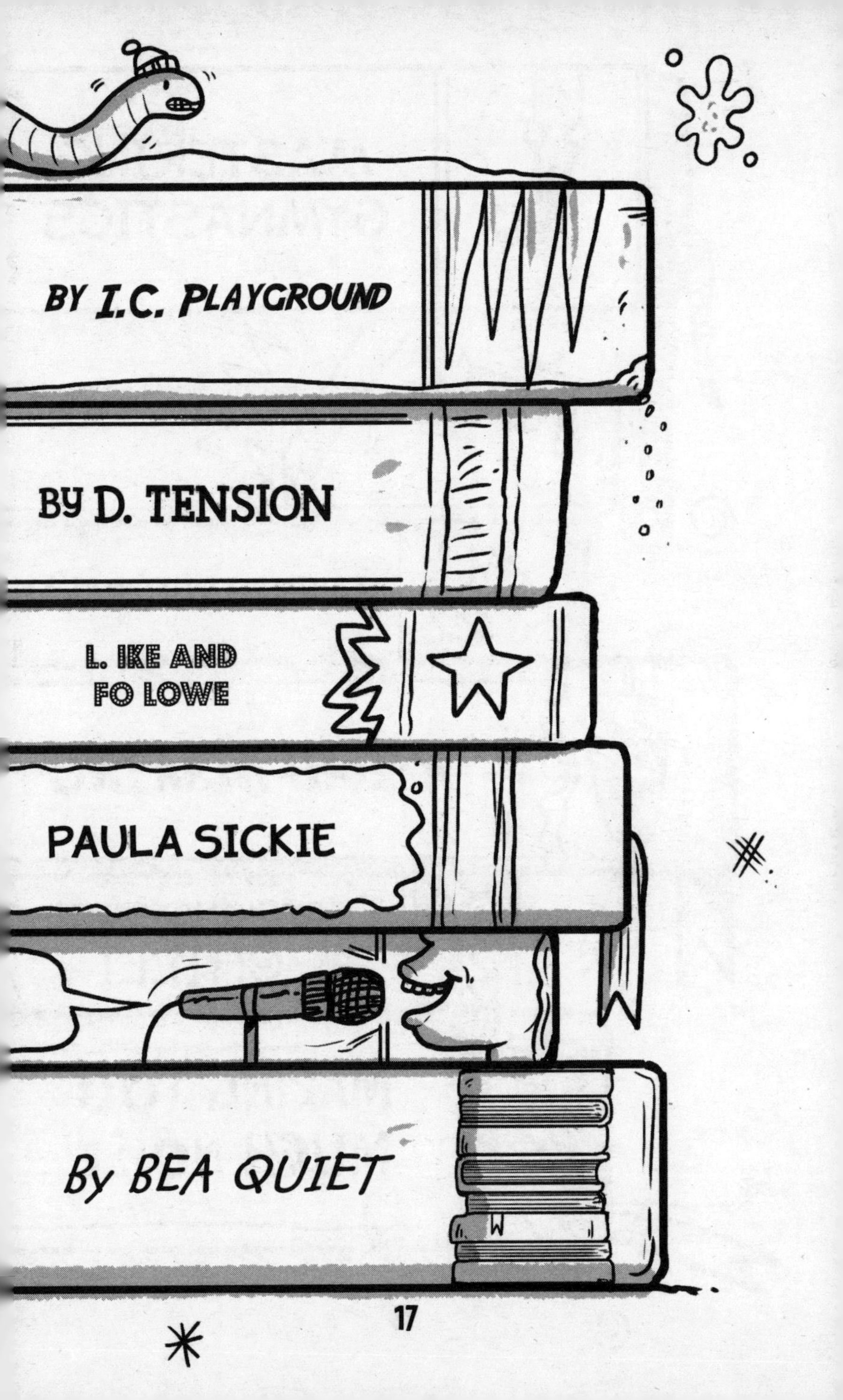
BY I.C. PLAYGROUND
BY D. TENSION
L. IKE AND
FO LOWE
PAULA SICKIE
By BEA QUIET

MASTERING GYMNASTICS
MAKING FRUIT SALAD
KEBAB MAKING
COOKING WITH CHILLI
MAKING TOO MUCH NOISE

BY BEN D. BODIE
DESPERATE FOR THE TOILET
BY NEIL E. POOPIN
CLEMENTINE SEGMENTS
&
MEL-ANN BALLS
BY PETER BREAD
BERNIE BUMBUM
ED ACHE

PRANKING YOUR MATES
by JOE KING
Carrying Books
by Ivor Backpack
Running Late for School
by Willy Getthere
Forgetting Your P.E Kit
M.T. LOCKER
HOW TO BEHAVE IN ASSEMBLY
Stan Still & Liz Zen
DISGUSTING SCHOOL DINNERS
by FI LINGILL

ENGLISH

English is very important for comedy because if you really want to get the best out of this book, being able to read would be a great help.

Similarly, spelling is crucial if you want to write a joke down, which you might have to do when the teacher has asked for absolute silence in class *(though once your friends have seen the joke, that will be even harder as they'll be finding it almost impossible not to laugh).*

However, one incorrect letter could spell disaster **(well, d-i-s-a-s-t-e-r spells disaster, but you know what we mean...).**

Take this joke for example:

Which food gets special treatment wherever it goes?

A V.I.Pea.

If your spelling wasn't that good and you wrote the answer as, **A V.I.Pee**, that would have quite a different meaning. I mean, it's not even food for one thing, it's more of a liquid, like a drink and... no, let's not go there.

The best thing about these jokes is that many of them involve clever wordplay, so if you get into trouble for making the class **LAUGH** too much during lessons, you can tell the teacher that the only reason you're able to make such good jokes is because you've been so well taught. Believe us, not only will you not get in to trouble, you'll get an **A****** , which is almost never given!

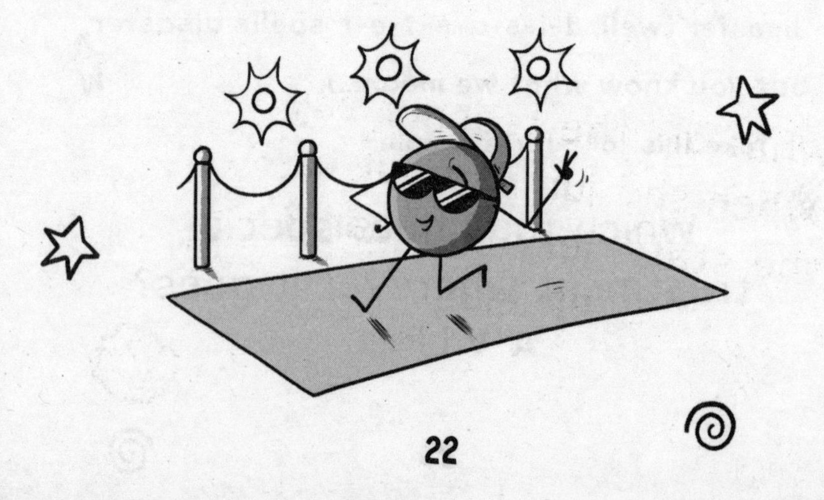

Why did the boy put a dictionary down his trousers?

He wanted to be a smarty pants!

I only know 25 letters in the alphabet. **I don't know y!**

What did the teacher say when she jumped out of the stationery cupboard?

SUPPLIES!

What's a wizard's favourite app?
Spell Checker.

Why did the boy bring flat pack furniture to school?

Because the instructions said it 'requires assembly'.

If an English teacher becomes an influencer are they an **InstaGRAMMAR?**

Girl: OMG! You just parped in front of the teacher!

Boy: Oh, I'm sorry. I didn't realise it was her turn.

Teacher: Why did you eat that gluestick?

Pupil: My lips are sealed.

What American insect is good with computers?

A U.S. Bee.

Teacher: Your grammar is very bad.

Pupil: Well every time she bends over she parps, but she means well.

Which word is always spelled incorrectly?

Incorrectly.

Which branch of the army is best at English?

The Essay S.

What type of dentist is good at writing?

An author-dontist.

What's the longest word in the English language?

Smiles – there's a mile between the first and last letter.

What is a pig's favourite play by Shakespeare?

HAMlet.

Teacher: Why have you written your essay on a banana?

Pupil: You told us to write a story on fruit.

Why is the punctuation mark at the end of a sentence never hungry?

Because it's a full stop.

I've just eaten all the Scrabble tiles!

The next time I poo, it could spell DISASTER!

What insect never writes a word incorrectly?

A Spelling Bee.

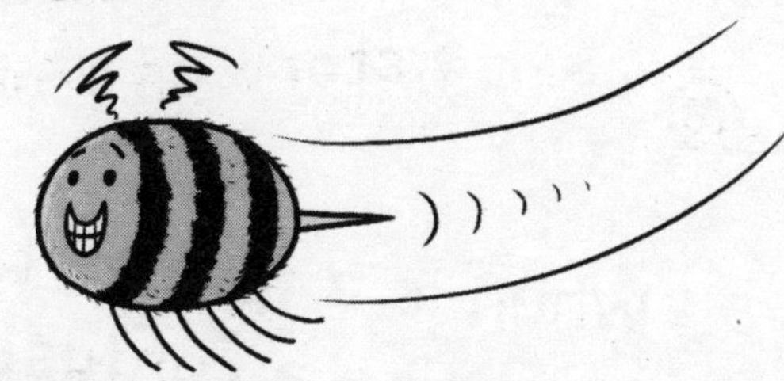

Which two letters in the alphabet are the oldest?

The second and third ones – they're always B.C.

Which letter of the alphabet is hard of hearing?

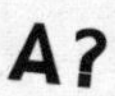

A?

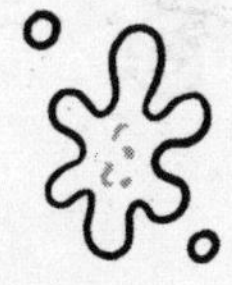

What's the yummiest letter in the alphabet?

Cream T.

When is a foreign language student like a confused camper?

When they use the wrong tense.

How much milk do punctuation marks like in their tea?

Just a dash.

Which two letters are most like a horse?

GG.

What do you win at the World Punctuation Championships?

An Apost Trophy!

Which award-winning British actor is a whizz at punctuation?

Colon Firth.

Why was Harry Potter top of the class in English?

He was great at Spelling!

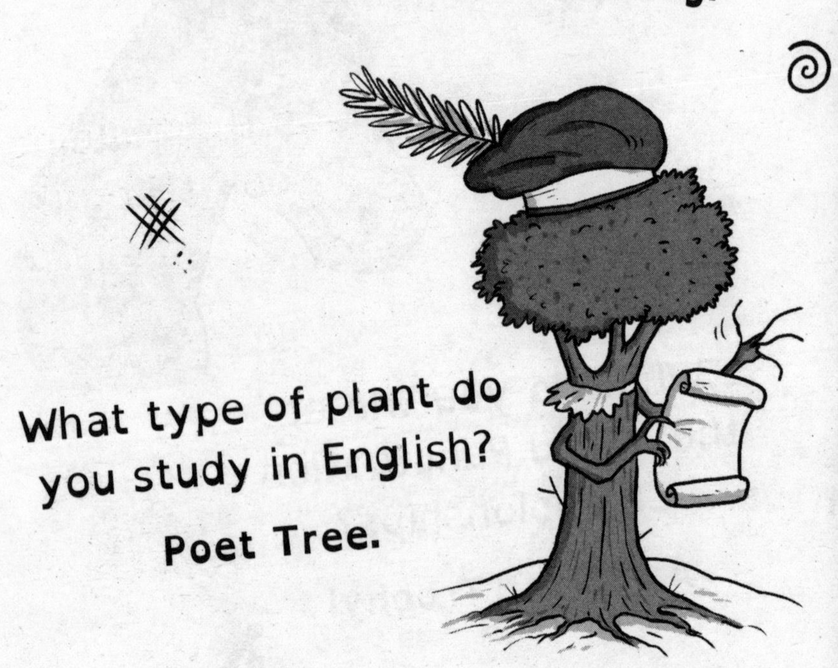

What type of plant do you study in English?

Poet Tree.

Pupil: Teacher, teacher, there's a violin in my book.

Teacher: Of course! All stories have a **beginning, fiddle, and end.**

Which pencil should I use to write my Shakespeare essay?

2B or not 2B? That is the question.

Why was the building like a book trilogy?

Because it had three storeys.

Why did the witch have to leave the school?

She was ex-spelled.

Is there **another word** for synonym?

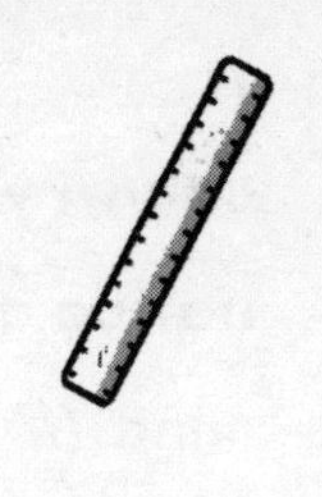

MATHS

In many ways, a joke is like a mathematical equation...

Set up + punchline = big laughs

But of course, it's not that simple. **(Maths rarely is.)** The set up needs to be delivered and explained clearly, the person you're telling it to needs to be awake and they have to be able to speak the same language. Then, the punchline needs to make sense, be timed perfectly and crucially, it needs to be **FUNNY**.

You also have to consider the age of the person you are telling it to *(under three and they're unlikely to get it)*, what they're doing at the time **(if they're taking part in a cross**

country race, or sitting on the toilet, it might not be quite appropriate) and their state of mind *(it's generally not a good idea to tell a joke to someone who is crying their eyes out because their younger sister has just stepped on their new phone and smashed the screen).*

So, now the equation looks like this...

{{(Set up/clear)Awake}/English + (Punchline x make sense)/timing/funny} divided by Age x activity x state of mind = big laughs

But **(you knew there was going to be a but, didn't you?)**, the actual size of the laughs also depends on a number of other factors. How loud the surrounding area is *(telling gags on a roundabout during rush hour is going to make it very hard to hear them)*, how many

people you tell the joke to *(you'd think the more people you tell it to, the bigger the*

laughs, but no, some laughs cancel others out so it's far more complicated than that) and whether or not someone parps just as you say the punchline **(this can be very confusing as people often laugh at parps, so you wouldn't be sure exactly what they are laughing at).**

So, our final equation looks like this...

**{{(Set up/clear)Awake}/English +
(Punchline x make sense)/timing/funny}
divided by Age x activity x state of mind
= big laughs – noise x number of people
divided by parp.**

There. So concludes your first lesson in algebra**hahahahaha...**

Teacher: If I gave you two dogs, and John gave you two dogs, how many dogs would you have?

Pupil: Five.

Teacher: No, listen carefully. If I gave you two dogs, and John gave you two dogs, how many dogs would you have?

Pupil: Five.

Teacher: No, no, no! Why do you keep saying five?

Pupil: Because I've already got a dog!

Teacher: If I have two tomatoes, three carrots and a cucumber, and I cut them all into three pieces, what do I have?

Boy: A salad?

How many maths teachers does it take to change a light bulb?

Sum.

Why was the maths teacher sad?

Because they always had problems to solve.

Why did a million trillion get a detention?

Because it was very nought-y.

What do you call a man with a calculator on his head?

Adam.

Teacher: If I have 30 children in class on Monday and 20 children in class on Tuesday, what do I have?

Pupil: A chickenpox outbreak?

Why should you always trust a calculator?

Because you can count on it.

Why were four, five and six scared?

Because seven eight nine.
But 7 was worried two, four six eight ten!

What's the hottest sum in the world?

Sum-mer.

How do you find the square root?

Under the square tree.

How many months have 28 days?

All of them!

Which knight invented circles?

Sir Cumference.

What type of food is like subtraction?

A takeaway.

What food is the best at doing sums?

Add-vocado.

What do you get if you take four chairs away from five?

A lot of people standing up.

Why are the mode and median the nicest averages?

Because the other one is mean.

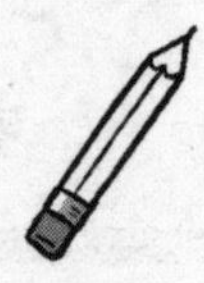

Teacher: If I gave you £100 and the headteacher gave you £100, what would you have?

Pupil: A brand new bike.

What do triangles, circles and squares do when they are unfit?

They get into shape.

Why is 90 degrees never wrong?

Because it's a right angle.

Which newspaper is very good at multiplication?

The Times.

Teacher: Who did their homework?

Pupil: Me Sir – it's bedside, kitchen, coffee and bird.

Teacher: What are you talking about?

Pupil: You told me to learn my tables.

What is the most musical part of maths?

Song division.

Why are detectives not very good at maths?

Because when they're investigating a crime, they often say, 'This doesn't add up'.

What rapper always does things by halves?

50 (per) cent.

Religious studies teacher: Why are you doing your times tables in my class?

Pupil: Because in the Bible it says, 'Go forth and multiply'.

What type of tree grows its leaves at right angles?

A geomeTREE.

If you freeze three cups of water would that make them **ice cubed?**

BREAKTIME

Ahh, the moment the sound of the bell fills your ears and you can all pack up your things and head outside. The fresh air! The freedom! The feel of wet grass between your toes! **Ahhhh...** hang on. Have you left your shoes and socks in the changing room again? Best go and get them and then pick this up when you are fully dressed.

The playground is the perfect opportunity to flex your comedy muscles but – as you'll have discovered by now – you have to pick your comedy moments carefully and you have to consider which groups of people you are approaching.

THE FOOTBALLERS

Every break, they are out there playing football – and they take their game seriously – so timing is everything. It's no good jumping out in front of someone to tell them a **HILARIOUS** one-liner just as they are about to score the winning goal. They won't find it funny no matter how well you nail the punchline **(though the other team might)**. Also, you have to consider, are you a football fan? If the only thing Messi in your life is your bedroom floor and the only Dele you care about is the one that sells the fully loaded, foot-long sandwiches then it's best to steer well

clear of any football jokes. Finally, the reaction of your audience will largely depend on who has won the game. Head for the winning team, they will be much more receptive to a fantastic pun than the losers.

THE GOSSIPERS

One thing you need to be aware of is that the gossipers only care about one thing. Gossip. So, there is some good news and bad news. The good news is, that we've analysed this group and totally understand that your jokes must be directly connected to the subjects of:

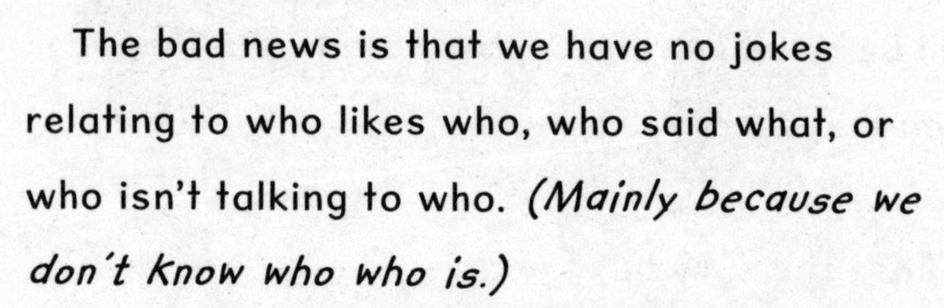

Who likes who.

Who said what.

Who isn't talking to who.

The bad news is that we have no jokes relating to who likes who, who said what, or who isn't talking to who. *(Mainly because we don't know who who is.)*

So, when they are all sitting together deep in conversation or hunting in a pack – sorry, we mean walking around the school – then it's best to avoid them. However, when they are on their own, then they are perfectly lovely people and you have the ideal opportunity to charm them with your wit and wisdom. Though whatever you do, don't tell them anything about your private life, or if you like someone, because it will go round the school quicker than Usain Bolt on a bullet train.

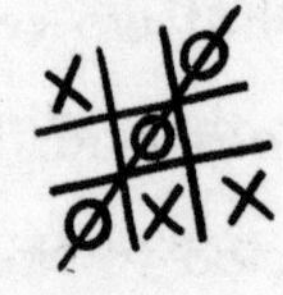

THE GEEKS

These are very busy people. They spend their breaktime swapping, comparing and discussing the latest fad. For this reason, your jokes need to be totally up to date at all times. Don't Panic. We've got your back! *(Not literally, otherwise you'd just be a pair of legs, a bum and a head.)* Nearly all the jokes are 100% brand new **(we've thrown in a few classics but only if they've passed our really complicated and thorough laugh test).**

So go ahead, approach the geeks, they are nice people who are just really passionate about things like films and collectables and gaming and coding. Who knows? They might become really passionate about your jokes!

THE ODD SQUAD

Firstly, you need to understand that the people in this group are now called 'alternative' or 'edgy' and it's cool to be weird and they may look super serious and take selfies whilst pulling really moody faces, but underneath there is a sense of humour – probably. It may take some work to actually find it, but it will be totally worth it when you manage to bring all the sub-groups together *(and the sub-sub-groups, though don't bother with the sub-sub-sub-groups, they're too far gone)* in one big comedy hug **(by the way, don't actually**

try and hug this group – they don't look like huggers to us).

So now we have the groups all sorted, it's up to you to arrange the jokes accordingly and go out there and give them the **FUNNY!** But, be quick, the bell will ring in a few minutes.

Knock knock.

Who's there?

The interrupting headteacher.

The interrupting headtea—

NO RUNNING IN THE CORRIDORS!!!!

What toy can you only use once?

A yolo.

What do birds play during break?

Hide 'n' beak.

What did the boy say when someone tried to take his building blocks?

LEGO, they're mine!

What playground game do computer geeks like best?

IT.

Who looks after the school at Halloween?

The Scaretaker.

What happened to the fly on the school toilet seat?

It got pee'd off.

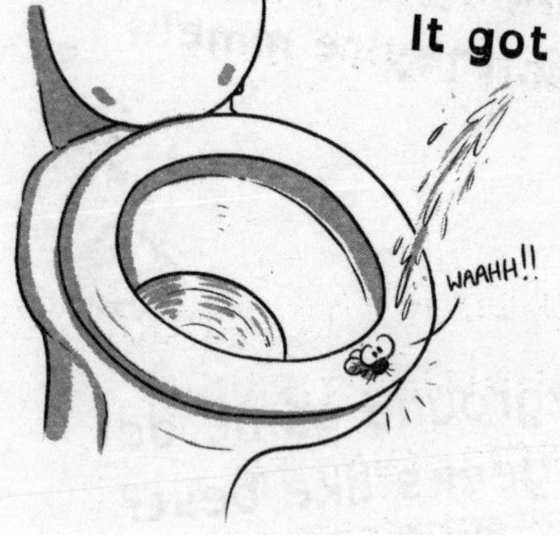

What happened to the boy who keep breaking wind in school?

He was sent to the bottom of the class.

What should you never play at school?

Truant.

Teacher: For World Book Day this year, Johnny came dressed as Where's Wally –
we still can't find him!

What do you do if the school bins start chatting to you?
Ignore them, they're talking rubbish.

Teacher: Why are you wearing swimming trunks?

Pupil: Because you said it was wet playtime.

What's a police officer's favourite playground game?

COPscotch.

What do you call a boy with a telescope on his head?

Luka.

What do you call a girl with an aeroplane on her head?

Skye.

What do you call a girl with a fire alarm on her head?

Belle.

What do you call a boy with grass on his head?

Mo.

What do you call a girl with a TV on her head?

Ariel.

What do you call a girl with a beefburger on her head?

Patty.

What do you call a boy with a lion on his head?

Rory.

What do you call a boy with a toilet roll on his head?

Louie.

What do you call a kid that never ages past 19?

Constantine.

What do you call a boy with a pile of hay on his head?

Bailey.

What do you call a boy with a farm on his head?

Barney.

What do you call a girl with diamonds and rubies on her head?

Julie.

What do you call a boy with a fish on his head?

Finn.

What do you call a girl that you can't find?

Heidi.

Being funny in a foreign language is tricky, which means it's often better to fall back on non-verbal funnies such as blowing a raspberry *(funny in almost any language, but not Flemish)*. However, here's the thing -

What is the thing, Ivor?

I'm coming to it, Steven, okay?

Woah, easy big guy, I'm just curious.

... everyone in the class is in the same boat-

Why are you talking about boats, Ivor?

I'm not! It's...look, just wait.

...they're all English speakers learning another language, so your jokes can still be in English,

comprenez vous? No of course you don't, which is exactly the point; you don't have to be fluent, semi-fluent or even un-fluent *in* a foreign language to make jokes *about* foreign languages, which is great for us because our German is *nicht sehr gut*, our Spanish is *muy malo* and our Italian is *inesistente*!

Look them up, Steven!

How did the Spanish teacher travel to Spain?

Si.

What is the shiniest language?

Polish.

What language do birds speak?

Winglish.

What, all birds?

No, some speak Flynese.

What language can you eat?

Danish.

What language is never spoken at night?

Day-nish.

But we just did a Danish joke, Ivor.

I know, Steve, but this is a different one.

What language do oranges speak?

Mandarin.

What language do chickens speak?

Hengali.

What should you do to make sure you're saying the right thing in Prague?

Czech.

And if you're still not sure?

Double Czech.

Where do they speak French?

From their mouths.

Teacher: What's your favourite language game?

Pupil: Hide 'n' Greek.

How do elks communicate?

Moose code.

What language do bossy teachers speak?

Demand-erin.

What language does everyone in the lunch queue speak?

Really Hungarian.

I got on really well with a dolphin on the school trip to the aquarium.

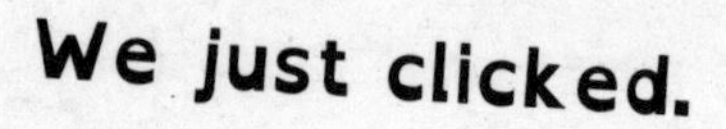

We just clicked.

SCIENCE

Scientists love a gag. Einstein would often say to people, **'Why is a family gathering a lot like my theories? *Because it's all relatives.'*** Marie Curie would tell her friends that when she discovered Polonium she was ***in her element,*** and Isaac Newton said that the reason he spent so long on the toilet was because ***he was working on his laws of motions***. So if some of the greatest scientific minds of all time liked a laugh, then there's no reason why you shouldn't tell a few jokes in class.

In fact, if it's in biology and someone **LAUGHS** their head off, the teacher could make your homework learning how to put it back on again. Remember though, as Newton taught us, for every action there is an equal and opposite reaction, so if you end up making the whole

class **CRY WITH LAUGHTER**, the chances are that the teacher will also be crying – though possibly not with laughter. Really though, what you're doing is conducting an experiment to see how many jokes it takes to cause uncontrollable giggling, but tread carefully, because if you add too many into the mix, the whole school could collapse in an ***EXPLOSION*** of laughter!

Why was the light bulb so awesome?

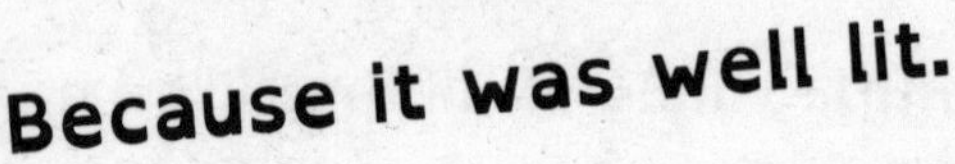

Why did the used battery give away neutrons?

Because they were free of charge.

What do you call it when an amoeba takes a picture of themselves?

A cell-fie!

I just read a book called 'Experimenting with Helium' –

I couldn't put it down!

Why didn't the physics teacher and the biology teacher go on a date?

Because there was no chemistry.

What is the silliest element?

Twitanium.

What social media platform do polar bears use?

ArcTicTok.

How does an astronomer organise their holiday?

They planet!

Did you hear the gossip about Oxygen and Magnesium?

I was, like, OMg!

Did you hear about the boy who stayed up all night studying for a blood test?

He got an A+.

Which science is best for children with sensitive skin?

NON-BIOlogy.

What was the Welsh biology teacher called?

Dai Sect.

Where do cows go to learn?

The Moo-seum.

Teacher: What is Einstein's third law of relativity?

Pupil: It's the one after the second law.

Why didn't the pupils take lessons about Sir Isaac Newton seriously?

Because they didn't understand the gravity of the situation.

Where do astronauts study?

In LUNAversities.

Why was Charles Darwin spinning in a circle?

He was explaining his theory of r-evolution.

Why are electric cars so expensive?

Because they charge a lot.

How did the science teacher cure bad breath?

With experiMINTS.

Teacher: What job would you like to do when you are older?

Pupil: Sleep all day – it would be a dream job!

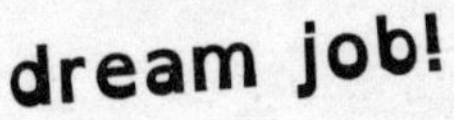

COMPUTING

Lessons about computers should be fun right? Except they want you to learn stuff and never let you play games, unless they are games which are designed so you learn stuff and all you actually learn when you play them is that you don't like playing games where you are supposed to learn stuff.

But it is the perfect opportunity to remind everyone that you are the **FUNNIEST** kid in the school and if you send the jokes via email then you can't even be told off by the teacher for talking. Plus, if your friends laugh out loud then they're the ones who will get into trouble, not you! It's a **win-win** situation!

All that really matters in these lessons is that the rest of the class learn that you are the funniest kid in the school and that means you

need to take Ctrl and Cmd, hit them with some Alt comedy so they ⏎ to school every day expecting you to deliver the ***#funnies.***

How do babies learn things?

They look it up on GaGaGooGoogle.

What computer is like a famous singer?

A Dell.

Why did the computer teacher wear glasses?

To help improve her webSIGHT.

What's the Pope's favourite games console?

NUNtendo Switch.

What's a Rabbi's favourite games console?

Pray Station 5.

Why wasn't the computer teacher at school?

She had a virus.

What type of computer does Jay-Z use?

A RAPtop.

What's the best app to listen to when you've got a cold?

SNOTify.

What do you do if your computer starts to cry?

Console it.

Which gaming character sells suitcases?

Pacman.

What's a chicken's favourite games console?

Eggs box 360!

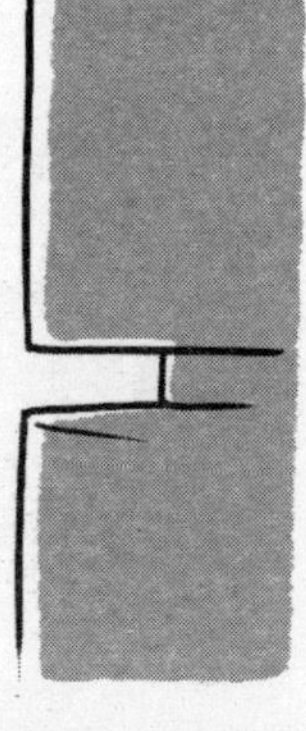

Why did the computer studies teacher quit teaching?

They couldn't hack IT.

What social media site keeps your breath minty fresh?

TicTacTok.

What is the best way to send a message to an insect?

Bee mail.

How does a computer eat an apple?

It takes megabytes.

Where do sheep share videos?

EweTube.

How did the influencer score the winning goal?

She kicked it internet.

Why did the pupil go to Brazil to get a book he needed?

Because he'd been told to get it from Amazon.

Why did the boy stop watching so many scary movies?

Because he was trying to cut down on his scream time.

What did the girl say after she got top marks in her computer studies exam?

Easy P.C.

SCHOOL DINNERS

Okay, there is danger here and not just because of the food that is often served up for school dinners. If you tell these jokes to someone who is eating, there is a ***strong possibility*** that the ensuing laughter will cause the food they are chewing to leave their mouth very quickly and, frankly, no one wants to get covered in half-chewed sausages, mash and lumpy gravy.

So it is best to take precautions:

- Full body armour is preferable, though that might make eating a little difficult for you.
- Using a **MEGAPHONE** so that you can tell the joke from a safe distance is a good idea, though then the chances are that everyone in the dinner hall will hear it and that could lead to a disaster not seen since the great food fight at St Cuthbert's High School back

in 2007. (They are still finding bits of half-chewed carrots stuck to the ceiling to this day).

- A good option is a sturdy clipboard. This is relatively small and can be quickly moved in to a protective position, though it might be worth acquiring one that can be easily wiped clean.
- The most important thing is to be prepared. Getting a **BIG LAUGH** from a joke feels great, but getting splattered in cold custard and soggy jam pudding afterwards does put something of a damper on things.

YOU HAVE BEEN WARNED!

Why are cooks scary?

They are always beating eggs, whipping cream and roasting potatoes.

Why are school dinners like a history lesson?

Because you might discover ancient grease.

Why was the boy eating a number?

It was one of his five-a-day.

How did the comedian get a job as a school cook?

Because the food tasted funny.

What is the school cleaner's least favourite pasta?

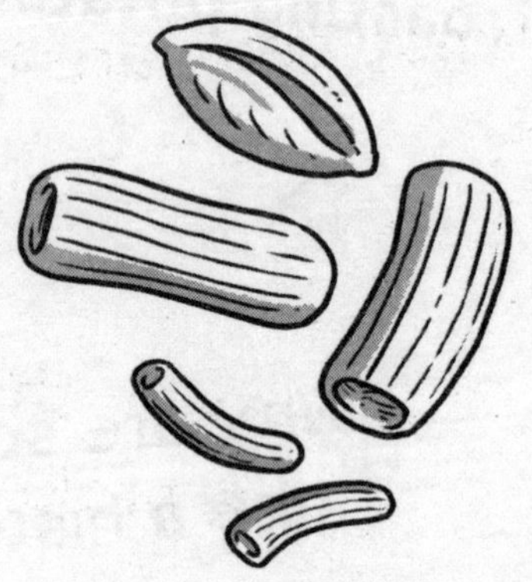

Muckarone.

If all the school cooks share cooking utensils does it become a Pots and PANdemic?

What is the German teacher's favourite pasta?

Berlin-guine.

What's the worst cake to get with your school dinner?

A stomach cake.

What peas are brown and sticky?

Poopeas.

Why was the potato like a broken plate?

Because they were both chipped!

What room has no windows or doors?

A mushroom.

What do you get if the school cook is hard of hearing?

Jelly and mustard.

Why is it so easy to have dinner at school?

Because it is handed to you on a plate.

What is a fork's favourite TV show?

Prongs Of Praise.

What is the music teacher's favourite Italian meal?

JAZZagne.

What did the knife and fork say when it was time for dessert?

We'll see you spoon.

*

What food thinks it's the best?

Boast Potatoes.

Pupil: These biscuits you gave us keep saying nice things to me!

Teacher: Well, they are complimentary.

Why does the weather presenter always check the menu?

Because if beans are on the menu, it could get very windy.

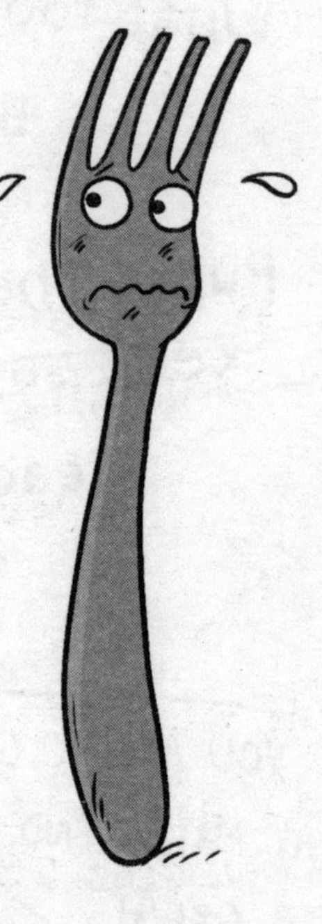

Why was the fork embarrassed?

Because he said the prong thing.

Why was the cutlery only used once?

Because after lunch it was all washed up.

What does a pig use to eat with?

A knife and pork.

Why were the girl's sandwiches missing from her lunch box?

It was a hacked lunch.

If dessert is sometimes called 'afters', why isn't the main course called 'befores'?

Why would the children only eat their lunch off a window sill?

They were ledgetarians.

What is the fastest food?

Runner beans.

What food do you have to wait the longest for?

Queue-cumbers.

What fruit always comes in twos?

Pears.

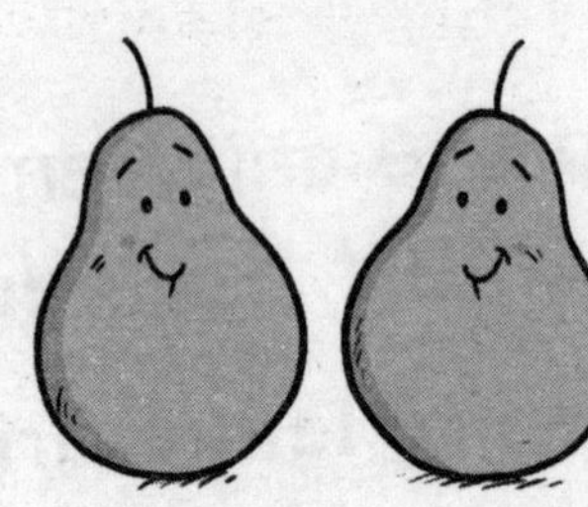

What type of jokes should you tell at lunchtime?

Cheesy ones.

Why did the bottle of lemonade keep falling over?

It was a dizzy drink.

Or should this be, it was a dizzy fizzy drink, Steve?

I don't know, what do you think Ivor?

But I asked you, Steve?

Yes, you did and then I asked you.

Thanks Steve, you've been a great help.

Any time, Ivor!

GEOGRAPHY

Geography is a cool subject – you learn things about different countries, mountains, ox-bow lakes... It's like going on holiday, except there's no beach or nice food or swimming or even those big ice creams with flakes in them...

Oookay, it's absolutely nothing like going on holiday. In fact, sitting in a geography class learning about loads of fantastic places is agony because it makes you wish you were in those places whereas, in fact, you're in a stuffy classroom and there are still four hours until hometime **(and it's probably raining).** So how can you alleviate the boredom? By telling **JOKES!** Before you know it, you'll be laughing about land masses, giggling about glaciers and tittering about tributaries!

Does your friend know any really cold places in North America?

Hold on, Alaska.

What's the funniest subject?

GeogLAUGHy.

What happened when you climbed the big tower in Paris?

Eiffel over!

Who travelled around the world in 80 days feeling sick?

Bilious Fogg.

Why was the horse worried about climate change?

Because she thought it was caused by a foal in the ozone layer.

What environmental organisation is dedicated to saving vegetables?

Greenpeas.

Teacher: What's the capital of Bulgaria?

Pupil: B.

Why was the girl so anxious about the environment?

She was an eco-worrier.

Why are wind turbines so popular?

They have huge fans.

Mountaineer 1: I can't believe it's so cold and snowy here on the Mount Everest. You told me the weather would be lovely.

Mountaineer 2: No, I said it would be a great climb, mate.

Where do pirates come from?

AARRRRRRR-Gentina.

Teacher: How many oceans are there?

Boy: Three – Oceans 11, Oceans 12 and Oceans 13.

Teacher: Why would you need a vegetation belt?

Pupil: To hold up your vegetation trousers.

What nationality are you when you complete a computer game?

Finnish.

Why do Australian children work so hard at school?

So they get their koala-fications.

Why are the people in Iceland so friendly?

Because they have some lovely geysers there.

What is the best thing to wear during a storm?

Thunderwear.

If you ride your bike to your friend's house more than once is that considered re-cycling?

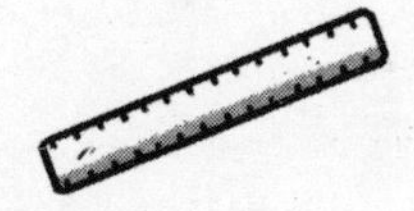

Why is Geology so cool?

It rocks.

Pupil 1: The bed in the hotel I stayed in, in South West France had really rusty springs in the mattress.

Pupil 2: Dordogne?

Pupil 1: Yes, that's exactly what it sounded like.

Pupil 1: My friend went to Budapest.

Pupil 2: Hungary?

Pupil 1: Yes, he was, but he found a restaurant eventually.

Pupil 1: I went to see an opera in the Far East.

Pupil 2: Singapore?

Pupil 1: No, she was quite good actually.

Pupil 1: I took my pet to the insect Olympics in the Caribbean recently.

Pupil 2: Antigua?

Pupil 1: Yes, she was really keen!

Pupil 1: I bought some lovely clothes in the Channel Islands.

Pupil 2: Jersey?

Pupil 1: No, mainly trousers.

Teacher: Can you find a Scandinavian country on the map?

Pupil: Norway.

Teacher: Well, you could at least try!

HISTORY

History would be great if it wasn't so old fashioned. When you study historical events, you'll notice they are often gory, shocking, disturbing and violent – but ***rarely*** funny – so that's where you come in. It's time to ***guffaw*** about before, bring some ***comedy gold*** to the chronically old and give ***mirth*** to the middle ages. That way, you can turn bygone days into bonkers days, bring some ***hilarity*** to history and maybe even turn Attila the Hun in to **Attila the Pun!**

With these gags you can forget about the past because, in the future, your name will go down in history as the funniest kid in school. In years to come, pupils will study you and say, *'That kid sounds like a comedy legend'*, or something.

What ended at the start of 1066?

1065.

Who was the sleepy leader of the French Revolution?

NAPoleon.

Which historical explorer loved to play tennis?

Serve Walter Rally.

Which monarch from the 16th century was always performing comedy sketches?

Mary Queen of Skits.

In which subject did the teacher only want to talk about his early life?

HIStory.

Teacher: Name one ground-breaking invention from all of history?

Pupil: The shovel?

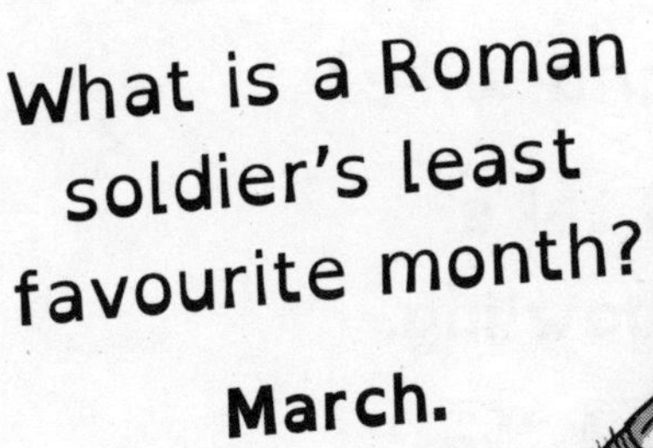

What is a Roman soldier's least favourite month?

March.

Which 19th century mathematician would have hated Velcro?

Ada Lovelace.

Why did the Roman woman never win at hide and seek?

Because Julius Caesar.

How did Henry VIII entertain his second wife?

He'd take Anne bowling.

What's the best thing to use for Roman arts and crafts?

A pair of Caesars.

Why did the history teacher quit his job?

He couldn't see any future in it.

How did Florence Nightingale get around?

In a LAMPorghini.

Who discovered Wotsits?

CRISPopher Columbus.

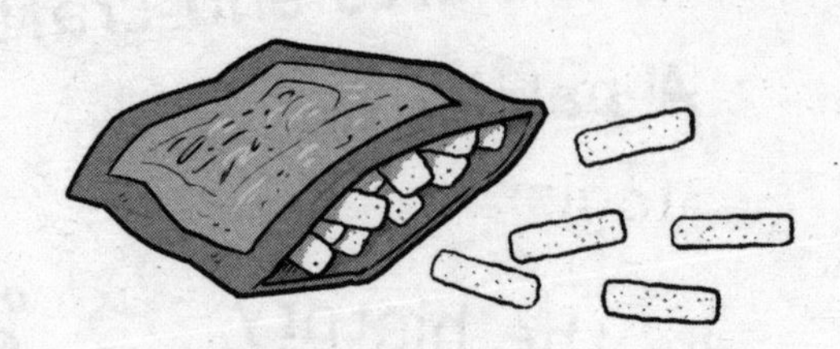

In history, who first invented the rules of tennis?

The Roman Umpire.

What did Julius Caesar tell his football team to do?

Mark Antony.

Why was the history teacher always talking about the Victorian era?

It was her favourite PASTime.

What is the correct name given to dogs that dig up bones?

Barkeologists.

Where did the Armada get its supplies?

Spainsbury's.

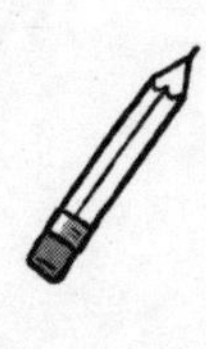

Why was the queen only 30cm tall?

Because she was a ruler.

Who was the most useless leader of the Mongol Empire?

Genghis Khan't!

What was Shakespeare's favourite computer game?

Sonnet the hedgehog.

P.E.

It doesn't matter what you do in P.E. – it could be football, netball, dodgeball, golfball, tennisball, boxingball, swimmingball or ballball – an opportunity could arise for you to bring out the comedy. When it does, you should make it your goal to seize that opportunity and run* with it *(but not too far – as when you tell the joke, they might not be able to hear it).*

*Or swim with it/skip with it/hop with it/crawl with it/climb with it/jump with it/star jump with it/burpee with it – depending on what you are actually doing in P.E.

Teacher: Your trainers are on the wrong feet.

Pupil: No, these are definitely my feet.

Why was the P.E. class so shocked?

Because the teacher made them jump.

Why do babies make great football players?

Because they are always dribbling.

My favourite exercise is a cross between a lunge and a crunch.

It's called lunch.

Why was the funniest girl in class so quiet in P.E.?

Because she'd forgotten her P.E. wit.

What's a pirate's least favourite exercise?

The plank.

Why did the student get so angry while she was running?

It was a cross-country race.

P.E. Teacher: I'll need a note from your parents if you're not doing PE today.

Pupil: Okay... laaaaaaaaaa!

P.E. Teacher: What was that?

Pupil: It's the note my parents gave me – C sharp.

Where do P.E. teachers keep their lesson plans?

In an exercise book.

What are the best exercises to do in space?

Star jumps.

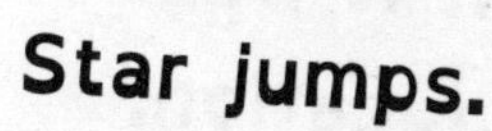

Why are footballers so inspirational?

Because they always aim for their goals.

What exercise lesson takes place in the toilet?

Pee E.

Why did the medium turn up to P.E.?

She thought it was Psychical Education.

Why do bogies like team sports?

They always get picked.

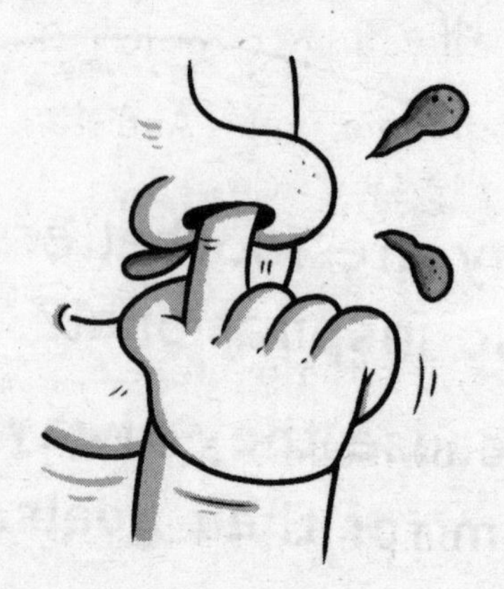

ART, MUSIC & DRAMA

Three subjects for the price of one now and all of them lend themselves to telling great gags and not getting into trouble.

Drop a ***rib-tickling gag*** in Art which has the class cackling their pants off and, if you film it, you can tell the teacher you are creating an NFT, a Non-Fungible Token, which is all the rage in the Art world at the moment, though beyond knowing that NFT stands for Non-Fungible Token, we have ***no idea*** what they are.

In Music, all you have to do is form a band and then sing some gags. And if you can get the class to **LAUGH** in time and in tune with the music, you may even get quite good marks. As for Drama, it's the perfect opportunity to work on your own show, a **GAG-TASTIC** spectacular complete with lasers, a mind-

blowing light show and amazing costumes. Failing that it could just be you standing in front of the class in your uniform, but either way we give you a cast iron guarantee* that, if you use these gags, your performance as a comedian will get you an A+ and quite possibly an Oscar.

So, get learning your lines, limbering up your tonsils and doing whatever it is you have to do to get ready for Art because your audience awaits and they are hungry for gags. **(They only had a small pun for breakfast.)**

*Though, just to be clear, any guarantees given in this book are not legally binding and may in fact be something we have made up on the spot because it was the first thing that came in to our heads.

What instrument gives you a winning smile?

A tuba toothpaste.

What did the shop assistant say when the boy bought a hip hop album?

Would you like it rapped?

What composer is the easiest to pick up?

Handel.

What did Beethoven's dog do?

Bach.

What has 20 feet and sings terribly?

The school choir.

Why was the printer so musical?

The paper was jamming.

Mum: I'm worried about Poppy. She's always at the theatre!

Dad: It's just a stage she's going through.

Why did the donkey lose its role in the nativity play?

It refused to reHORSE its lines.

Which painting is always complaining?

The Moaner Lisa.

What do Santa's helpers like to paint?

Elf portraits.

What pop band were the best at drama when they were younger?

The Script.

Why was the robber unhappy that her picture was in the art gallery?

She didn't like being framed.

Who is a police officer's favourite artist?

Constable

What did the police officer say when he walked past three members of the orchestra's string section?

Cello, cello, cello.

What do you get if you mix red, green, yellow and blue paint together?

Messy.

What did the sculptor say when his brother knocked on the door?

Statue, bro?

Why should the person who gets the main part in a play have a good appetite?

They're given a big roll.

Which pop star spends a lot of time in bed?

Lazy Gaga.

What singer is also in charge of a school?

Head Sheeran.

Why was the star of the school play so relaxed before the opening night?

She didn't want to make a drama out of a drama.

Which part of an orchestra is it best not to sit too close to?

The wind section.

Who is the stinkiest Hollywood actor?

Bad Pitt.

Teacher: What's your favourite opera?

Pupil: Opera Winfrey.

Who got the main part in a play about a farm?

The lead tractor.

What is a fish's favourite play?

A Midsummer Night's Bream.

SCHOOL TRIPS

School trips are the best. Well, in theory they are the best, but in practice you have to get on a stinky school bus and sit in traffic for hours and hours and when you do get to the museum **(or wherever you are heading)** you are told you can't run really fast and slide across the hall on your knees *(fun)* and instead you have to be really quiet and fill in a bunch of worksheets *(not so fun)* and the only thing to look forward to is the gift shop at the end which is really, really expensive and where, if you are lucky, you can just about afford a pencil, rubber or a badge.

So, to make the trip worthwhile, what everyone needs is a good laugh. Think of it as your duty to turn a museum into an ***amuse-eum.***

Very good, Steven!

Thank you, Ivor.

Don't mention it.

I didn't, you did...

The good news is there are plenty of opportunities to unleash the funnies. The coach or school bus is ***perfect.*** Then there is the queue to get in to wherever you are going. Then there is lunchtime, when you realise the packed lunch you brought is nothing to smile about. Soggy sandwiches, crushed crisps and a warm drink. **JOKES TO THE RESCUE!**

Teacher: Why are you leaving the museum with that statue?

Pupil: Because I'm taking the bust home.

Where can you learn about chemistry, physics and biology but you need to be really, really quiet?

The Silence Museum.

Where did the class go to learn about coprolites?

The Poo-seum.

Where do ghosts go on their school trips?

Boo-seums.

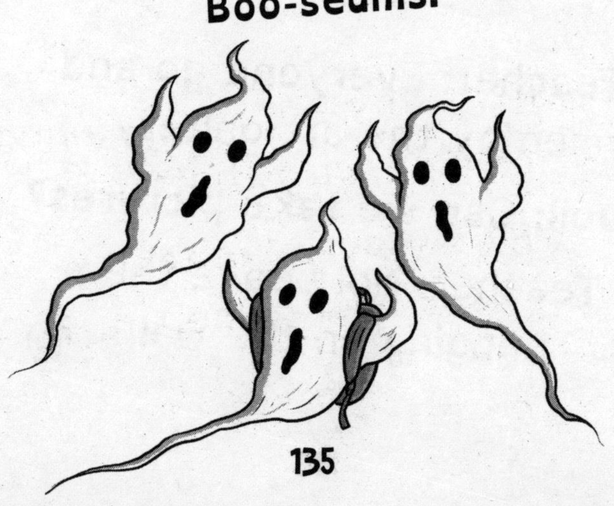

Why couldn't the librarian go on the school trip?

It was overbooked.

Teacher: Everyone go and enjoy the art gallery

Pupil: Can we take pictures?

Teacher: No! Leave them hanging on the wall!

Teacher: This term we will be visiting the recycling museum.

Pupil: I've heard it's just rubbish!

What's the best way to arrange a successful class trip?

Tie all their shoelaces together.

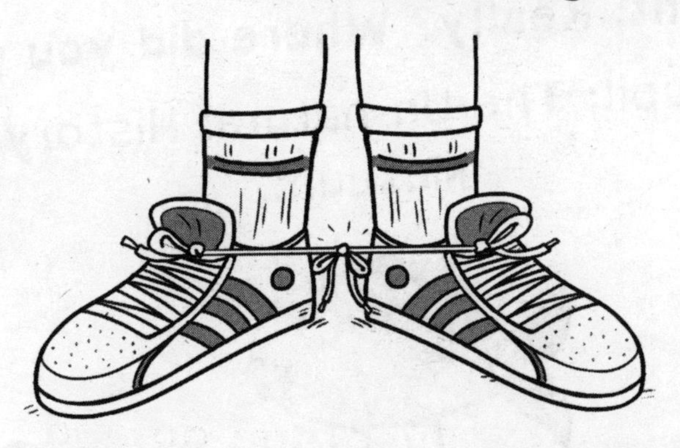

Why did the teacher bring a piece of paper covered in black and white squares to the school trip?

It was her check list.

Teacher: Did you enjoy the school trip to the farm?

Pupil: No, it was a load of crop.

Pupil: We saw a fish with legs, a goat with wings and a bright green elephant on our school trip today.

Parent: Really? Where did you go?

Pupil: The Un-natural History Museum.

What are horses' favourite trips?

Field trips.

Teacher: How was your trip to the trampoline park?

Pupil: It had its ups and downs.

Teacher: Stop whacking the ground with that big stick and get onto the bus.

Pupil: But you said it was time to hit the road.

HOMETIME

Every good comedian knows that it's important to send your audience home **LAUGHING**.

However, this can be tricky when you're telling jokes in school as your audience might have just scorched off their eyebrows with a bunsen burner, or they may have just had to sit in detention for something they didn't do – their homework perhaps! So they might not be in the ***best*** mood for a joke. If the mood of your audience isn't great, then that means it's going to take some really, ***really*** good jokes to get them laughing.

Well, fortunately you have a ***bucketload*** of belters primed and ready to go right here in this book, so the moment the bell rings, **GET GAGGING!** *(As in, telling jokes... not puking!)*

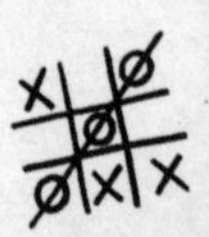

Why did the pupil start brushing their hair at the end of the school day?

They thought it was comb time.

What animals always turn up at the end of the school day?

Homing pigeons.

What herb do pupils like best?

Home thyme.

On the way home from school today, town was really busy....

I went into the shop selling school bags.

Packed!

I went into the chemist for some cold medicine.

Congested!

I went into the shop selling balloons.

Bursting!

I went into the shop
selling snooker
equipment.

Cued!

I went into the shop
selling marmalade.

Jammed!

I went into the doctors to
see about my tummy ache.

Cramped!

I went into the shop
selling cream cakes.

Desserted!

Why were the two schoolkids like famous films?

Because one walked Home Alone and the other one walked Home Alone 2.

Why did the boy who loved pudding want to stay at school?

Because he heard there was an 'afters' school club.

Parent: Why are you doing maths in a bubble bath?

Child: I'm doing my foam-work.

Why did the pupil go to 221B Baker Street at the end of the school day?

Because she thought it was Sherlock Holmes time.

Teacher: That's the end of the day, time for you to go home.

Pupil: But I'm home schooled.

Teacher: Then it shouldn't take you long to get there.

At the end of the school day, why did the pupil sit in their garden holding a fishing rod and wearing a red, pointy hat?

They thought it was gnome time.

Why is going home on Friday like the punchline to a bad joke?

Because of the weak end.

Parent: Why aren't you doing your homework?

Percy: Because I don't live here and I'm a cat.

I know this is a bit strange but I quite like it.

OK, Ivor, but it is a bit weird.

I know, Steve, made me laugh though.

Me too.

OK, let's leave it in for the readers who are a bit strange too.

Like us, Ivor?

Yes, like us, Steve.

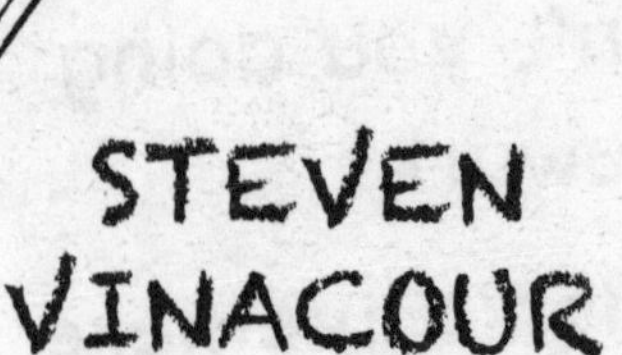

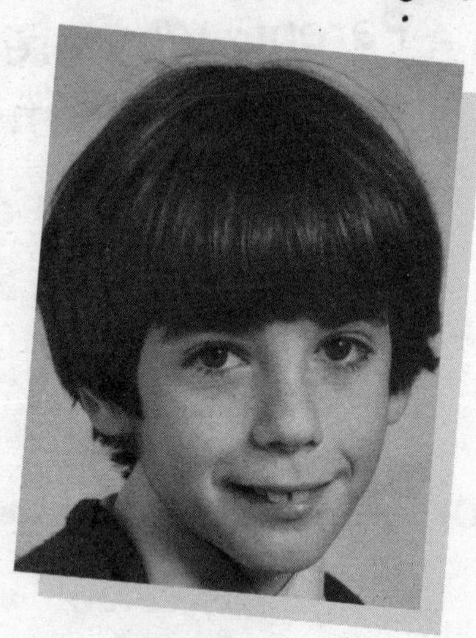

Steven started his comedy career about 600 years ago as a jester for Henry VIII. He entered a new talent show, 'Tudor You Think You Are?', but came second to a woman who juggled bagpipes!

He can often be heard shouting 'knock knock', but usually only after his family have locked him out for telling too many jokes. He has been voted the world's funniest writer 136 times (by his mum).

He now sits alone and writes the **Ted and His Time-Travelling Toilet** series, occasionally surfacing to run an award-winning production company, writing and directing commercials.

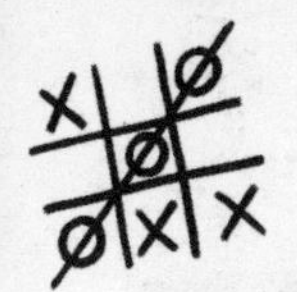

IVOR BADDIEL

Ivor has wanted to write jokes since he was 10 years old. That was when he broke his foot and received a letter addressed to 'I've A Bad Heel'. He laughed his head off, which, with a broken foot as well, meant he was in a bad way, but he soon recovered.

Since then, he's written jokes for lots of TV shows and quite a few books, and thinks that if you get this book, you won't be saying, 'I've a bad deal,' you'll be saying, 'I've a very good deal.'

ALSO BY STEVEN VINACOUR...

ISBN 978-1-78270-384-6

ISBN 978-1-78270-385-3

Don't miss **Ted's** ***AMAZING***

TIME-TRAVELLING TOILET

ADVENTURES!

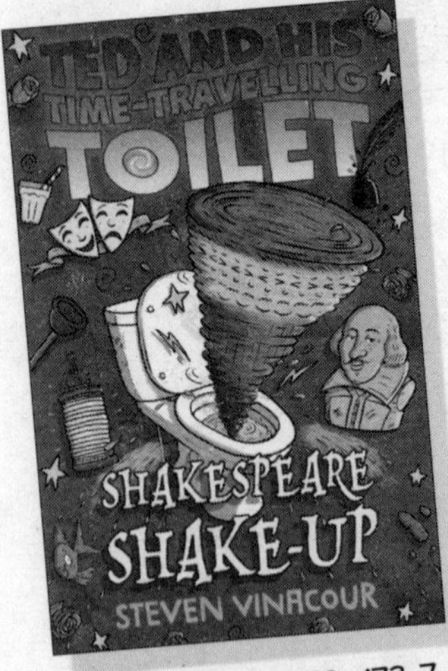

ISBN 978-1-78270-473-7

ISBN 978-1-78270-476-8

TED AND HIS TIME-TRAVELLING TOILET

ROMAN REWIND

Turn the page for a **sneak preview** of ***TED'S*** whacky and wonderful world of **TOILET TIME-TRAVELLING**. One flush and you're **away!**

CHAPTER 1

I'm Ted and I have a secret. Actually, I have two secrets. The first one is just a normal, ordinary secretive kind of secret. The other, on the scale of secrets, with one being a teeny, tiny little secret and ten being the most humungous, jaw-dropping, pant-wettingly enormous secret – this is definitely a ten... and a bit.

If I were to come straight out and just tell you the secret then it's possible that the shock of hearing it could cause your head to pop off your shoulders like a cork from a bottle. I would feel very guilty if that happened to you and I'd have to answer very ANGRY emails from your parents telling me that I caused your head to pop off, fly out the window, land on a passing lorry and be carried off never to be seen again. No one wants that.

So, I'll start by telling you the little secret first and we will just have to see how well you cope. First you have to promise never to tell anyone...

... promise?

... really promise?

... really, really, really promise?

OK, I'll tell you. Come a bit closer ...

... closer ...

... even closer ...

THAT'S TOO CLOSE!

Back up a bit.

Too far ...

Take half a step forward ...

Hmmm... take a quarter of a step

backwards.

There... stop... OK. Now, before I tell you, you also have to promise that you won't laugh. You won't, will you? And when I say laugh I also mean giggle, chuckle, chortle, cackle, snigger, smile, guffaw and titter.

All right then. Ready?

Shhhhh...

Here goes...

My name isn't really Ted!

I know, right? Mind blowing!

Let me explain.

I re-named myself Ted as soon as I turned ten. I decided on Ted because it was the shortest name I could possibly think of which was the exact opposite of my real name which, thanks to my parents, is the stupidest, most ridiculously long name in the whole entire world. They decided to name me the most stupidest, longest, most ridiculously long name in the whole entire world because they thought it would give me character. In fact, all it gave me was a sore hand whenever I wrote my name on my homework! So, if you promise not to laugh I will tell you my full name ...

... promise?

Really, really, truly, hand-on-heart promise?

OK, here goes...

My full name is Terry Barry Larry Gary Harry Jerry Perry Lenny Benny Johnny Tommy Julie Jones.

Are you laughing? Because you promised not to.

The problem is that my parents are hopeless at making decisions. Some nights they spend so long making up their minds what they want for supper that it's time for breakfast. So, when my mum was pregnant with me, they made a list of all the names they liked and then couldn't decide which one to give me, so they gave them all to me. At that time, they also didn't know if I was going to be a girl or a boy. If I turned out to be a girl, I would've just been named Julie as that is the only girl's name they liked. When I turned out to be a boy they felt it was a shame to waste such a lovely name (bleugh) and so they put it on the end. Typical isn't it? The only quick decision they ever made and it was the wrong one!

The last time I heard my full name was when I got myself into trouble for 'accidentally' repainting my school trousers. Grey is such a boring colour and I thought green stripes would work this season. When I noticed that I'd also managed to get green paint all over my bed sheets, I knew I'd be in double trouble. So, when my mum stood at the bottom of the stairs with her hands on her hips and shouted, 'Terry Barry Larry Gary Harry Jerry Perry Benny Johnny Tommy Julie Jones, come down here at once!' I knew what was coming.

I didn't move. She called again and again. Finally, she marched up the stairs and burst in through my door knocking over a pile of comics I'd just sorted out.

'Why didn't you answer me when I called?' she shouted.

I pointed out her mistake at once.

'You missed out Lenny.'

'What?' she replied.

'You missed out Lenny. My name is Terry Barry Larry Gary Harry Jerry Perry **Lenny** Benny Johnny Tommy Julie Jones, and you said Terry Barry Larry Gary Harry Jerry Perry Benny Johnny Tommy Julie Jones, which technically isn't my name so I couldn't be sure that it was me you were calling.'

Mum stood in the doorway counting out

my names on her fingers. I waited for her to realise that she had made the mistake. I went back to reading my comic until she had figured it out.

'Right, well anyway... You are in big trouble, young man. What on earth were you thinking? Painting your school trousers with green stripes? And you've ruined your bed sheets!'

'I was being creative, Mum. I was thinking outside the box.'

'What box?' asked Mum.

'The box, not a box,' I explained. Mum scratched her head and looked confused.

'You don't have a box.'

'I know, but if I did... ' I replied.

'But you don't!' she argued.

'BUT IF I DID!'

'How big is it? Where would you keep it? Your room is full of junk. Put the junk in the box.'

'What box?' I asked.

'The box?' she said.

'What box?'

Now we were both confused about the box that we don't have, and Mum had completely forgotten why she came upstairs in the first place so I avoided getting told off about the green striped school trousers.

Now, let's move on to the second secret. This is the big one. And when I say big, I mean

BIG!

In order for me to tell you, we are going to have to go somewhere completely safe where no one could possibly hear what I say. I was thinking under my bed or in my wardrobe, but if Mum comes in again and finds me hiding in my wardrobe or under my bed with a complete stranger, then questions are going to be asked. So, there is only one option left. You take this book somewhere quiet and double-check that no one is listening then I'll tell you.

It's OK, I'll wait...

Ready?

Double-check again that no one is listening. Just in case. OK, here goes... I have a **TIME-TRAVELLING** toilet!

Shhhh!

Don't say anything. Just let the pant-dropping awesomeness of what I just told you sink in slowly and then I'll tell you all about it in a little while.

Sit down, calm down, maybe even go to the toilet. You know, your normal, ordinary non-time-travelling toilet. Unlike mine which is time-travelling.

Did I mention that?

Oh no, you've become all excited again.

Sit down (again). Calm down (again).

I'll be back in a minute...